Vanishing Georgia

PHOTOGRAPHS FROM THE

VANISHING GEORGIA COLLECTION,

GEORGIA DEPARTMENT OF ARCHIVES AND HISTORY

Vanishing Georgia

THE UNIVERSITY OF GEORGIA PRESS   ATHENS

Library of Congress Cataloging Data

Georgia.   Dept. of Archives and History.
    Vanishing Georgia.

    1. Georgia—Description and travel—Views.
2. Georgia—Social life and customs—Pictorial
works.   3. City and town life—Georgia—
Pictorial works.   I. Title.
F287.G27   1982   306'.09758   82-4764
ISBN 0-8203-0628-2   AACR2

90 89 88   5 4 3

This book is affectionately dedicated to Carroll Hart,
director of the Georgia Department of Archives and History
from 1964 to 1982.
Throughout her eighteen years as director,
Miss Hart devoted her life to preserving the state's
historical records for all Georgians.
It was she who first recognized the rich potential and value
of the historical photograph,
and it was her vision and determination that made possible
the Vanishing Georgia program.

*The photographs in this volume are from the
Vanishing Georgia Collection.
The text was written by Sherry Konter
and the prints were made by George S. Whiteley IV
from negatives in the collection.*

Contents

Acknowledgments

The Vanishing Georgia program has been such a rewarding experience for the Archives staff that we have wished there were some way we could share it with the people of the state who contributed so much to its success. By bringing together a selection of photographs from the collection we hope to convey our pride in what has been accomplished and our gratitude to everyone who has helped along the way.

We also want to express our thanks to the many local societies over the state and their members who were so helpful in carrying word of Vanishing Georgia to the people of their counties. We could not have succeeded without you.

To Dr. Margaret Child of the National Endowment for the Humanities, whose faith in Vanishing Georgia encouraged us to pursue the program—and, indeed, made it possible—we say again, thank you.

Our administrators, former Secretary of State Ben Fortson and the present Secretary of State, David Poythress, gave us the encouragement and support we needed to carry the program forward.

Governor George Busbee, an avid photographer himself, made it possible for us to continue the program when federal funding ended.

We would like to acknowledge the contribution of George Pearl, the first Vanishing Georgia coordinator, and that of Lynn Meyer, former assistant to the present coordinator, as well as the help given the project in its early stages by volunteers from the American Institute of Architects Auxiliary.

We would also like to thank Karen Bouffard, Ed Bridges, Emily Calhoun, Paulette Cochran, Elizabeth Fitzpatrick, Marian Holmes, Elizabeth Knowlton, Sam Mahone, Gail Miller, and Virginia Shadron for their cooperation and assistance in the preparation of this book.

We are particularly indebted to George Whiteley, our photographer, who has been with Vanishing Georgia from the very beginning and who helped in the selection process in addition to making prints of all of the photographs reproduced here. His expertise and dedication are gratefully acknowledged.

And to all of you throughout the state who have shared with us your stories, your photographs, and your memories, we are deeply grateful. Working with you has been one of the special rewards of the program.

Sherry Konter
Coordinator, Vanishing Georgia

Introduction

The words "Vanishing Georgia" worry the imagination. What is vanishing? Tired old houses, moss-covered trees, quiet vistas along a country lane, fields white with September cotton, people waiting at the depot to meet the train? To each of us the words conjure up a different scene. In some of us they evoke a feeling of nostalgia, thoughts of a way of life that has disappeared or is fast disappearing. For others they may serve as a reminder, perhaps even as a bitter reminder, that the "good old days" were not always so good. Above all they remind us that things change, that time passes.

The archivist has the responsibility of capturing the memory of a people and preserving it so that future generations can know how it was in the past, what people thought, how they lived, how they amused themselves. This is a grave responsibility. Which record shall be preserved and which destroyed? In an attempt to capture the spirit of a people, to record the fragile heartbeat of a society, the archivist is always seeking better means of documentation.

For many centuries the written word has been the principal medium for recording human activities. Archival records have been in existence since man ceased his wandering and camped long enough to be counted and taxed. From the clay tablets of Ebla to the video tape of the first shuttle through space, information has been recorded which reflected the happenings of the period.

It is strange that until fairly recent times the archivist seemed almost unaware of the value of the photograph as a historic document. Images were present in many repositories, but they were seldom catalogued and little thought was given to their protection. Nor was much effort made to seek out and preserve those which would eventually turn to ash in the smoking city dumps of America. Librarians began to develop photograph collections, but they too were slow to appreciate the value of these arti-facts—and they lacked the proper techniques to ensure their protection.

Yet the photograph has been available to us for almost a century and a half—since 1839, the year Louis Jacques Mandé Daguerre announced to the world that he had discovered a process for capturing an image on a thin copper plate coated with silver. It is difficult for us now to grasp the enormous impact that Daguerre's art had. Daguerrian galleries blossomed and people who could not afford to have their portraits painted hurried to these galleries to have their pictures taken. By the end of the 1850s other processes had replaced the daguerreotype, but the photograph—whether on silver, glass, sheet iron, or paper—was to remain with us.

From the beginning there were photographers in Georgia, the earliest of them itinerants who came for a few days or weeks, announced their arrival in the columns of the local newspaper, and then moved on to an-other city. But some of these stayed. Soon they began to move out into the smaller communities, so that photo galleries were commonplace by the middle decades of the nineteenth century. Among these early Georgia photographers were R. L. Wood, one of the first to practice his art in Macon; A. J. Riddle, also of Macon; Isaac Tucker, J. W. Perkins, and George J. Gable in Augusta; John Woodbridge in Columbus; C. W.

Motes in Athens and later in Atlanta; R. J. Nunn and T. T. Wilmot in Savannah.

Much of the work of these photographers survives as portraits, many of their subjects unidentified and unidentifiable. The photographer himself is frequently unknown to us in the case of the images made before 1860. Some, however, left views—Tucker and Perkins, for example, and photographers like J. N. Wilson and O. Pierre Havens of Savannah who specialized in stereoscopic photography. Several examples of the stereoscopic art appear in this volume.

The pictures in the Vanishing Georgia Collection span the history of photography—from daguerreotype images to snapshots made by amateurs holding box cameras. Most document the period 1890 to 1930. The pictures are chosen primarily for their documentary content and historical significance.

The program was begun by the Department of Archives and History in 1975 as a pilot project with almost no funding. Its purpose was to preserve for posterity some unique aspects of the Georgia experience by going into the field and copying photographs in the possession of individuals, historical societies, schools, churches, and businesses. These early contacts demonstrated beyond any doubt that the program would be enthusiastically supported. The National Endowment for the Humanities partially financed the program for two years, after which state funds were made available for its continuation.

The Vanishing Georgia program has developed a network of citizens who are interested not only in the preservation of photographs but in other aspects of their local heritage as well. The staff coordinator visits the county seat about two months before the scheduled arrival of the team. She shows photographs, explains why they are significant, and presents the logistics for the development of a successful program. She also assists in the choice of a central location for the Archives bus which serves as a photographic laboratory.

The Vanishing Georgia team usually spends two days at a location. Participants bring in their pictures, which are photographed and returned to them. They give identifying information and receive instructions on how to preserve, store, and identify their pictures. Two copies are made of each photograph selected. One negative becomes the security copy and is stored in a special vault under optimum environmental conditions. The other negative becomes the working copy. Each picture is assigned a number.

The prints reproduced in this book were made from copy negatives, and in each case the identifying number is given in parentheses following the caption. Unfortunately it was not possible to include photographs from all of the 159 counties in the state. The limitations of space dictated otherwise. Even if space had not been a consideration, geographical coverage in the book must necessarily reflect coverage within the collection itself, and there are counties yet to be visited. There are also counties that the Vanishing Georgia team will no doubt want to revisit at some time in the future. We do, however, believe that the photographs brought together here suggest the great wealth of the collection.

Vanishing Georgia

The Land

From its very beginnings Georgia was to be a land of hard-working farmers. The Trustees for Establishing the Colony of Georgia in America—a group of prominent Englishmen who requested, and were granted, a royal charter—designed the colony to supply products that the mother country could not easily obtain elsewhere. The Trustees enacted laws prohibiting slavery and rum and laws regulating the Indian trade in order that Georgia would develop as a land of yeoman farmers. Though these laws were soon relaxed, Georgia—like the other southern colonies—became a state whose people were bound ever so tightly to the land.

The lowlands of the coast were found suitable for growing indigo and rice, and soon landowners bought and brought slaves to work the marshy fields. Planters from Virginia and North Carolina moved into the Georgia upcountry to try out their tobacco crop on fresh soil. But the most momentous event of all occurred in 1793 with the invention of the cotton gin, a development that in many ways determined the fate of the state, the region, and the nation. With the invention of the gin, cotton came to dominate the southern economy for the next 150 years.

Georgia was indeed an agrarian state, but by and large it was not a culture of landed gentry. The *Gone with the Wind* society existed much more in the pages of a novel and on a Hollywood movie set than it did on

Georgia soil. Before the Civil War as well as afterwards, the majority of farmers had only themselves and their families to work their land and to plant and harvest their crops.

Although cotton was indisputably "king," many other crops were grown in different sections. Farmers raised cattle, sheep, and swine in the pine-barrens and wiregrass areas, and those in the rocky northwest planted corn and raised livestock. Apple orchards dotted the fertile valleys of the northeast. Central and south Georgia farmers grew tobacco, sweet potatoes, sugar cane, wheat, oats, and peaches in addition to their cotton crop.

The industrialization of the 1850s and 1860s affected the rural areas as well as the towns and cities. Cotton mills, syrup mills, and grist mills sprang up throughout the countryside, as did tanneries, slate and marble quarries, copper and coal mines, sawmills, and turpentine distilleries.

Nevertheless, cotton stood above all else. The depression of the early 1890s forced farmers to attempt diversification. Many tried dairying, truck farming, and even the commercial production of watermelons and peaches. But as soon as the cotton prices improved, they returned to what they knew best. By 1916 cotton prices were higher than they had been anytime since the 1850s.

As cotton dominated the agrarian landscape, so did the sharecroppers, black and white, who worked land owned by others in return for a share of the crops they harvested—frequently a fifty-fifty arrangement. It was a system that gave a man some control over the piece of land he worked, but it was also a system that shackled whole families into generation after generation of poverty. Other farmers, cash-paying tenants and those who owned their land, enjoyed a better quality of life, though it was hardly a life of luxury.

Agricultural life in Georgia changed significantly during the 1930s. The boll weevil and the diversification programs of the New Deal hastened the decline of cotton and promoted the production of tobacco, peanuts, pecans, lumber, and livestock. The Rural Electrification Program brought electricity to thousands of Georgia farms, and other New Deal programs introduced farmers to better farming methods. However, between World War I and World War II more and more farmers left the land, seeking what they hoped would be a better life in the towns and cities. The move from the farms to the cities increased at an even greater rate following World War II, especially for blacks, and the dominance of farm life passed as Georgians adapted to the urban era.

GWINNETT COUNTY
Children picking cotton on the Carroll farm, 1908. (GWN-83)

COWETA COUNTY
Facing page: Cotton gin owned by W. L. Crowder, 1905. The Crowder gin was in the Handy community west of Newnan, also the site of a cane mill, sawmill, grist mill, and wheelbarrow factory. (COW-8)

WHITE COUNTY
The Helen Mine owned by Jarrett and Patton, ca. 1900. (STP-19)

LUMPKIN COUNTY
Corn-shucking on the farm of the London family south of Dahlonega, ca. 1890. One Georgian
described shuckings as "light-hearted frolics that made work seem play." (LUM-142)

9

LAURENS COUNTY
Timber rafting on the Oconee River, ca. 1890. (LAU-123)

MORGAN COUNTY
Facing page: The blacksmith was an important part of the community in the days when there
were wagons to be repaired and horses to be shod. (MOR-029-001)

MUSCOGEE COUNTY
Workers in a field near Columbus, early 1900s. From a picture postcard. (MUS-111)

BALDWIN COUNTY
Facing page: An early Georgia governor, David Mitchell, built this frame plantation house in the country northeast of Milledgeville in 1823. It was destroyed by fire in the 1940s. (BAL-66)

Women hulling rice with mortar and pestle. Sapelo Island, early 1900s. (SAP-93)

Facing page: Georgia cornfield, early 1900s. Many farmers grew corn, but it was never a major crop. (GEO-113)

HALL COUNTY
Tanner's Mill, said to be one of the oldest grist mills in the state. Early settlers hauled their wheat and corn to the mill to be ground into flour and meal. (HAL-252)

THOMAS COUNTY
Facing page: Workers gathering watermelons, ca. 1895. (THO-141)

PULASKI COUNTY
Steamboat taking on cargo on the Ocmulgee River at Hawkinsville. The cargo was probably turpentine. Georgia's pine forests produced lumber, but also rosin and turpentine. By the turn of the century there was one turpentine still for every sawmill. (PUL-3)

GLYNN COUNTY
Facing page: Schooners waiting to load naval stores at the dock in Brunswick, ca. 1890. In the late 1800s and early 1900s hundreds of thousands of barrels of turpentine and rosin were shipped from Brunswick and Savannah. (GLY-223)

LUMPKIN COUNTY
CCC (Civilian Conservation Corps) camp near Dahlonega, ca. 1934. In the depression years
of the 1930s thousands of young men took part in this federal program aimed at providing useful
work and vocational training while conserving and developing the country's natural resources.
(LUM-109)

GREENE COUNTY
Facing page: Abandoned farmhouse, 1941. This picture was one of a series taken by Farm Security Administration photographer Jack Delano. (GRN-25)

MORGAN COUNTY
Canning peaches on the homeplace of Marcellus Atkinson near the Brownwood
community, ca. 1914. (MOR-017-008)

JONES COUNTY
Facing page: Picking peaches on the Hunt farm near Round Oak, ca. 1910. With the introduc-
tion of new varieties, the peach had by 1890 become "the queen of Georgia orchard fruits."
(JON-35)

DEKALB COUNTY

Harvesting wheat on the Flowers farm, ca. 1910. The men are, left to right, E. W., Emmitt, and Marion Flowers. (DEK-2)

PAULDING COUNTY

Farm accident, ca. 1920. The transition from ox and mule to tractor was not always an easy
one. This farmer may in fact be awaiting the arrival of a team of mules to rescue his equipment,
whose weight was clearly too much for the wooden bridge. (PLD-8)

RABUN COUNTY

Rabun Gap, early 1900s. View from the Dickerson house looking across a cornfield to Wolf Fork Valley in the distance. (RAB-135)

RABUN COUNTY
Woman hoeing corn on her farm in the mountains near Clayton. (RAB-196)

On the following pages:

TROUP COUNTY
Left: Weighing cotton in the field, ca. 1933. Field hands were paid by the number of pounds they picked. (TRP-127)

COBB COUNTY
Right: Marietta, ca. 1890. Farmers who have brought their cotton to market fill the courthouse square. (COB-262)

FLOYD COUNTY
Workers at a sawmill in the timber near Rome, ca. 1909. The owner of the mill, Ben Camp, is the man standing near the saw at far left. (FLO-167)

GWINNETT COUNTY
Facing page: Sorghum mill near Yellow River, 1912. The mill was owned by Plesy Jones, the bearded man standing between the furnace and the evaporator filled with steaming molasses. (GWN-112)

GWINNETT COUNTY
Hanging beef for butchering, ca. 1905. The farmer and his family raised almost everything they ate. (GWN-7)

BEN HILL COUNTY
Facing page: Milking time, ca. 1895. In the late 1800s and early 1900s almost every farmer had at least a small dairy herd. (BEN-255)

On the following pages:

COWETA COUNTY
Left: Women of the Raymond Community Council grading and packing the first case of eggs marketed by the cooperative, 1921. (COW-1)

CHATHAM COUNTY
Right: Making a purchase at Hall's Wayside Market near Savannah, ca. 1940. Before the coming of the interstates, fresh fruit and vegetables from nearby orchards and gardens could be found along many country roads. (CTM-1)

The Town Evolves

Some prospered, some declined, some never seemed to change, and some even disappeared. But small towns, the slow pace, the attitudes, and the deeply held values they fostered have more than left their mark on the Georgia character. They developed as marketplaces, mill towns, boom towns, railroad stops, health springs, and resort communities. And so often they were home to generation after generation of the families who first settled there.

The earliest towns sprang up around Savannah, the state's first settlement, and spread southward along the coast. Before the coming of the railroads, rivers functioned as major trading and shipping routes and thus determined the evolution of the towns that grew up along them. Settlers moved up the Savannah River, establishing communities along the way. Later, in search of more fertile land, they moved inland, creating new towns which served as marketplaces for their tobacco and cotton and as gathering places for those newly settled in the area. With the discovery of gold in 1829, many a hopeful settler rushed to the rocky terrain of the north Georgia mountains. Though few found their fortune, some remained and began to raise sheep and cattle.

Beginning with the rise of the railroads, towns developed as junctions and distribution centers along the lines. Atlanta began as the terminus of one railroad and in fact was originally called Terminus. Settlers continued pushing into the western part of the state, building more and more communities.

The small towns of Georgia had much in common with other towns across the South. There was a main street along which one might find a drygoods store or two, a drugstore, barbershop, millinery, hardware store, gin, blacksmith shop, and perhaps even a photographer's gallery. And there was of course a depot and a post office. It was here that people came, both residents of the town and of the surrounding countryside, to purchase supplies, buy a new pair of shoes or a bolt of cloth, or simply to visit with the proprietor.

The town square was the center of activity, the great meeting ground, the focal point of community life. If the town were a county seat, here stood the courthouse, usually the largest and most imposing structure within miles. Men lolled on the grounds, sat on the steps, exchanged local gossip, and waited for the outcome of the trial in progress upstairs. People gathered on the square for special events and celebrations of all sorts. And they gathered here to listen to the promises of political candidates and to hear the latest word from Atlanta.

There were also the buildings that now stand as vacant testimony to busier days of years gone by: the opera houses and vaudeville theaters that provided entertainment to so many people in so many towns; the once grand hotels, with their lavish interiors and sumptuous ballrooms; the mill houses and stores, schools, and even churches which the company owned and operated; and the rustic resorts in pristine landscapes, health resorts where Georgians came to partake of the natural springs and mineral waters, or ocean communities where some of the richest men and women of America came to escape the bitter winters of the Northeast.

But as time passed, Georgia, like the rest of the country, changed. As early stagecoach routes gave way to railroads, as the railroads fell on hard times, so did the towns that served them. Boom towns lasted only as long as enough gold or other minerals could be found to warrant their existence. Mill towns closed when the textile companies moved elsewhere. And the resort communities suffered as people found new cures for their ailments, new places to vacation, and new ways of getting there.

By 1970 over 60 percent of Georgia's population had left the small towns and rural areas and moved to cities such as Atlanta, Macon, and Columbus which offered greater economic opportunity. At the same time, urbanization eroded many of the fundamental traditions of small-town life—the tradition of an extended, close-knit family living on the same land, perhaps even in the same house as their grandparents and great-grandparents before them, the tradition of a more relaxed and slower paced existence, traditions we remember as providing a stable, steadfast, and wholesome way of life.

RABUN COUNTY
Clayton, 1909. A horse-drawn hearse leads a funeral procession down muddy Savannah Street past mourners gathering on the wooden sidewalk. (RAB-125)

FULTON COUNTY
Facing page: This picturesque covered bridge crossed the Chattahoochee River to Roswell, ca. 1900. The Roswell Cotton Mills can be seen on the left and the Roswell Hotel, right. (FUL-160)

SUMTER COUNTY
The J. W. Harris & Company hardware store located on the corner of Lamar and Forest streets in Americus, 1880s–1890s. (SUM-129b)

WILKES COUNTY
Facing page: The old Wilkes County courthouse on the square in Washington, ca. 1890. The building was erected in 1817 and survived into the early 1900s. (WLK-142b)

On the following pages:

BIBB COUNTY
Left: Bricks were needed to build Georgia's towns and cities. This picture, from an 1876 stereograph by A. J. Haygood, shows the brickyard of William F. Anderson and Walter S. Ballard in Macon. (BIB-79)

FULTON COUNTY
Right: In the early 1890s this Atlanta grocery store was located on the east side of Whitehall Street between Hunter and Mitchell streets. The gentlemen with mustaches standing in the doorway are the proprietors, Robert Dohme and J. J. Duffy. (FUL-165)

RICHMOND COUNTY
Confederate monument on Broad Street in Augusta, ca. 1878. (RIC-178)

HANCOCK COUNTY
Facing page: Whatever the community, the church was at the center of community life and the growth of a town could be measured by the number of churches that were established. This photograph shows the old frame Methodist church in Sparta, ca. 1900. The building burned in 1905. (HAN-17)

On the following pages:

COLQUITT COUNTY
Left: This wooden structure located at Hartsfield, with the crudely lettered sign over the doorway, was not unlike other post offices throughout the state at the beginning of the century. The postmen carrying mail pouches and holding letters in their hands are ready to make their deliveries. (CLQ-175)

CARROLL COUNTY
Right: Rural mail carriers in Bowdon, 1912. Photographed before leaving on their routes are, left to right, P. C. Morris, George Downs, L. D. Hamil, Charlie Lovvorn, and W. B. Rowell. Carriers not only delivered mail but dispensed news, gossip, and other bits of local information as well. (CAR-19)

RANDOLPH COUNTY
Interior of one-room school, ca. 1900. Schools in larger towns were more spacious and offered better facilities. (RAN-207)

LAURENS COUNTY
Facing page: Two little girls on the front row in this picture hold a slate on which has been chalked "Bender School 1904." Typical of rural schools at that time, this one-room building accommodated all ages—although some of the people appear to be parents, not students. (LAU-159)

Facing page: This elegant mansion built in the 1850s by the wealthy Macon merchant and banker William B. Johnston still stands, but the way of life that made the fulfillment of so grand a dream is gone forever. *Left*: The spring house on the grounds of the Johnston mansion. Both photographs are from stereographs taken in the 1870s. (BIB-97, BIB-71)

The Gas Light Company and Columbus Railroad Company, located near the corner of
Broad and Twelfth streets, Columbus, ca. 1900.
The sign in the window advertises gas as "the
best fuel on earth." (MUS-34)

Facing page: Intersection of Eighth and Greene
streets in Augusta, early 1890s. The fire tower
was erected in 1860 and stood on the site until
it was dismantled in 1894. (RIC-186)

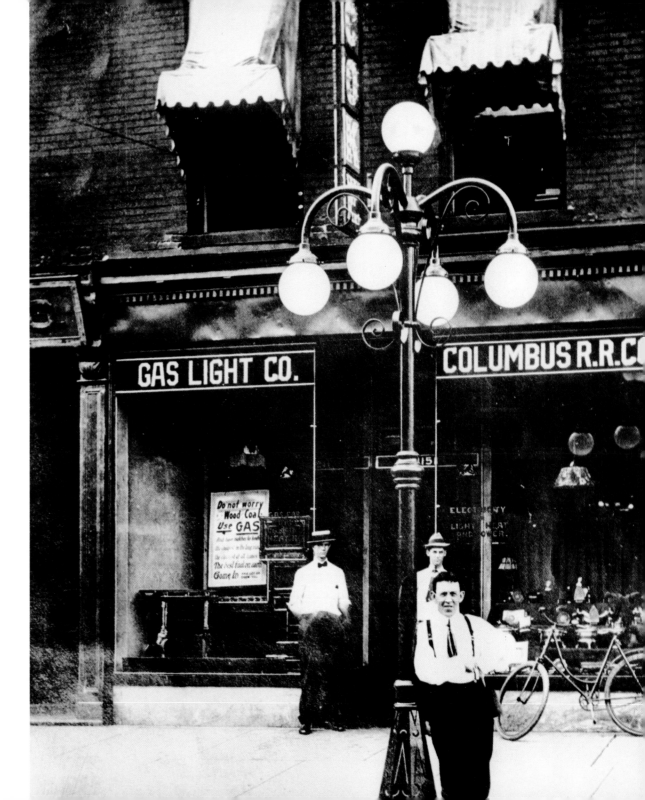

BROOKS COUNTY

Towns bypassed by railroads stagnated; towns on railroad lines flourished. This photograph taken in 1899 shows the main yard of the Georgia Northern Railway Company in Pidcock. Six years earlier the first train had made the run between Pidcock and Moultrie. (CLQ-70)

FLOYD COUNTY

Facing page: Rome, ca. 1890. This impressive brick building housed the Masonic Lodge, but also provided space for a dry goods store as well as for other business establishments, including a photographic gallery. In the window beneath the striped awning a display of the photographer's work can be seen. (FLO-83)

Photographer A. J. Haygood took this photograph of an express wagon drawn by oxen being loaded or unloaded on Cotton Avenue in downtown Macon. From a stereograph, 1876. (BIB-82)

Facing page: Barbershop owned by Frank Ramsey Pidcock, Sr., Moultrie, ca. 1915. Haircuts were 25 cents, shaves 15 cents, and for 10 cents the barber dispensed "hair tone." The signs reminded customers that all work was strictly cash and that no vulgarity of any kind was allowed, "as it might offend someone and is unpleasant for all." (CLQ-56)

CHATHAM COUNTY
Looking down Bay Street, Savannah, 1880s.
From a stereoscopic view by O. Pierre Havens.
(CTM-218)

CHATHAM COUNTY
Facing page: Bird's-eye view of the port of Savannah, ca. 1880. From a stereograph by J. N. Wilson. (CTM-217)

On the following pages:

LOWNDES COUNTY
Left: Many of the larger towns in Georgia had electric streetcars by the turn of the century. This Valdosta Street Railway Company car carried passengers to and from Pine Park. (LOW-52)

BEN HILL COUNTY
Right: Steamboats carried passengers and freight on Georgia's rivers. This photograph taken in 1898 shows the paddlewheeler *John L. Day* tied up to a loading dock on the Ocmulgee River. (BEN-81)

FULTON COUNTY
The Broad Street bridge looking west, Atlanta, 1870s. (FUL-647)

BURKE COUNTY
Facing page: Office of the *True Citizen* in Waynesboro, 1907. All except the smallest towns had a weekly newspaper. (BUR-159)

CARROLL COUNTY

Before the coming of the automobile, and for a while after, the delivery wagon was a familiar sight on the streets of small towns. This Villa Rica Electric Light & Power Company wagon delivered Coca-Cola. Villa Rica, ca. 1904. (CAR-171)

WILKES COUNTY

Interior of the Mary Willis Library in Washington, 1890. The library was founded two years earlier by Dr. Francis T. Willis as a memorial to his daughter, and gave the people of Washington access to a fine collection of books housed in an elegant Victorian building that few other Georgia towns could match. (WLK-50)

CHATHAM COUNTY

Savannah, 1911. Frank Dieter's Wholesale and Retail stall in the city market offered fresh meat, cut to the customer's specifications. (CTM-109)

MUSCOGEE COUNTY
Block of Broad Street in Columbus, 1904. (MUS-110)

BIBB COUNTY
U.S. post office at the corner of Mulberry and Third streets, Macon, 1894. The Victorian Gothic structure also housed a number of federal offices. (BIB-131)

MUSCOGEE COUNTY
Facing page: The Springer Opera House in Columbus at the turn of the century. Edwin Booth brought Shakespeare to the Springer, opera was performed here, and one writer called it "the cultural center of the Chattahoochee Valley." (MUS-125)

FULTON COUNTY
Union Station in Atlanta, ca. 1890. The carriages to the left of the picture are lined up along
Decatur Street. (FUL-330)

BEN HILL COUNTY
Facing page: Ice factory in Fitzgerald, early 1900s. (BEN-224)

BLECKLEY COUNTY
Snow and more snow, a surprising six and a half inches, lay on the ground in Cochran in 1901,
blocking passage of photographer Millard Fillmore Timmerman's photo car. The railroad car
was both studio and home for Timmerman. (BLE-4)

LANIER COUNTY

The lady in the buggy waits in front of the McMillan & McGee photo car on a railway siding in Lakeland, ca. 1890. This is the same studio on wheels later used by Millard Fillmore Timmerman, who remodeled it. (LAN-4)

BEN HILL COUNTY

An elderly gentleman with a cane, another gentleman holding a sword and scabbard, and other bystanders stare into the camera of J. C. Black, who was photographing this photo gallery in Fitzgerald, ca. 1905. (BEN-142)

LAURENS COUNTY

Facing page: Bread salesman Reuben Smith made his deliveries around Dublin in this wagon. (LAU-168)

BEN HILL COUNTY

View of Fitzgerald shortly after its founding, 1895. A woman who had come down from Missouri expecting to find a city of fine houses found instead "shacks built of rough lumber and not ceiled nor plastered." But shortly that began to change. "You can hear the hammer and saw in all directions from morning until night," she said. By 1899 the town had a population of 7,500 and the tents and shacks had been replaced by more permanent structures. (BEN-126)

MUSCOGEE COUNTY

Facing page: Office of Lucius Henry Chappell, Columbus, 1897. Chappell, shown seated at his desk, was in the real estate and insurance business. He was elected mayor the year this picture was taken. (MUS-152)

How We Looked

JONES COUNTY
Jesse M. Hunt and his wife enjoy a leisurely afternoon in the yard of their home, Hunt
stretched out in the hammock with a copy of
The Country Gentleman, Mrs. Hunt in a rocker
beside him sewing. The photograph, taken
about 1905, was used on the cover of a later
issue of the magazine. (JON-6)

We looked happy and we looked hopeful. We looked proud. We looked stern. The camera recorded it all.

In the early days of photography we went to the daguerreotypist's gallery to have our likeness captured on a thin coating of silver. We were arranged in formal poses, usually on a raised platform that faced the sun, our head held firmly in place with a clamp to prevent any movement. The exposure required anywhere from several seconds to several minutes, and thus very few of us attempted a smile.

Even later, when the exposure time had been reduced and the daguerreotype had been replaced by other processes, sitting for the photographer was more often than not a serious occasion. We were, after all, presenting ourselves as we wanted others to see us.

Some of us dressed for the occasion: the women in taffeta and silk, the men uncomfortable in stiff collars and suits saved for weddings and funerals. Others chose to appear as what they were: blacksmiths posed with their anvils, carpenters with their saws and hammers, ministers holding their Bibles; a railroad man liked to pose beside his engine. And there were the soldiers, whose likenesses might very well be their last ones.

Children were photographed in goat carts and wicker carriages, clutching dolls, riding rocking horses. The photographer could be depended upon to furnish appropriate props and to distract his subject at precisely the right moment. A painted backdrop showing a rural scene could be replaced in the wink of an eye by one showing a street scene or the drawing room of a mansion. We could stand on what seemed to be the back platform of a train, or we could appear to be rowing a boat, or even driving a car. We leaned against papier-mâché boulders, swung on make-believe gates, gathered studio roses.

Especially revealing are the family photographs taken by traveling photographers who passed through the county. Our families were larger then, frequently including grandparents, maiden aunts and bachelor uncles, and sometimes even cousins. We posed in our Sunday best on the porch or front steps of our home, or we loaded the family into our new automobile, especially if it were an open touring car that held seven people.

Sometimes we posed with some member of the family who had died, standing beside the casket or holding a dead child in our arms, a custom that now seems macabre but that was commonplace at a time when death was a frequent visitor. It was in fact so commonplace that photographers often advertised "portraits of the deceased" as one of their specialties.

Even when the portraits that fill the pages of family albums are not identified, and many are not, they have value as social documents. They frequently reveal our pride in who we were and what we had done. They preserve the smiles that boasted of a new dress, our first bicycle, the house we built, the friends we made, the family we raised. They record the styles we wore, the poses we assumed, and the expressions on our faces. Together they reveal not only how we looked but how we lived and how we thought.

Daguerreotype portrait of George Washington Lay, left, and his cousin James Berry Lay, ca. 1855. The earliest of the photographic images, the daguerreotype flourished in the 1840s and early 1850s, but had virtually disappeared by the 1860s. (GOR-477)

MONROE COUNTY
Elizabeth Ross, middle to late 1850s. The photographer who took this ambrotype portrait posed his subject before a painted backdrop. Unlike the daguerreotype, which was an image on a thin copper plate coated with silver, the ambrotype was on glass. The ornate gilded brass mat that frames this picture was typical of the period. (MNR-24)

FULTON COUNTY
Man with hat and cane, Atlanta, ca. 1885.
(FUL-352)

TROUP COUNTY
Facing page: One Victorian notion of fun was to dress up in fine plumage and strike theatrical poses. Photographer Kruger of West Point took this 1895 group portrait. (TRP-121)

MORGAN COUNTY

Earnest Willie, 1890s. Despite an accident that left him crippled, the young man who posed in his wheelchair would later become one of Georgia's most colorful figures. A fiery preacher and lecturer sometimes referred to as a cross between Billy Sunday and Carrie Nation, William D. Upshaw served several terms in the Congress from Atlanta and was a candidate for president on the Prohibitionist ticket. (MOR-6)

DOUGHERTY COUNTY

Facing page: The people in this photograph have obviously been carefully posed by the photographer—for example, the elderly gentleman in the rocker reading a newspaper, the two young girls seated on the downstairs gallery with open books in their laps, the ladies on the upstairs gallery. What we are seeing in fact is a portrait of a Victorian house and a Victorian household, ca. 1890. (DGH-54)

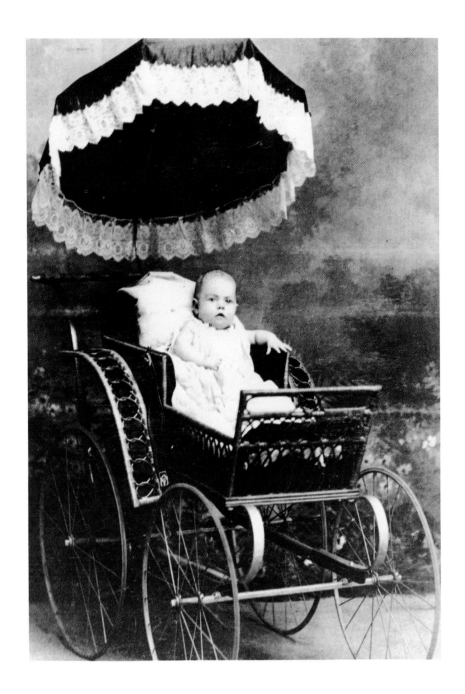

BIBB COUNTY
Baby in elaborate wicker carriage photographed in the studio of L. S. Hill & Company, Macon, ca. 1890. (LAU-56)

GWINNETT COUNTY
Facing page: Postmortem portrait, early 1900s. From the beginning of photography, likenesses of the dead were fairly common. This photograph of Trixie Davis, who died of "membranous croup" at the age of three, is unusual because it was taken outdoors. (GWN-97)

JOHNSON COUNTY
Girls with waist-length hair, ca. 1890.
(JHN-108)

HALL COUNTY
Facing page: Photographers often kept a supply of props to put into the hands of children. The little boy in the big coat is holding a riding crop. The little girl with the miserable look on her face is clutching what appears to be a folding camera. (HAL-67, HAL-83)

Confederate soldier, ca. 1863. This unusually clear ambrotype shows R. Harrison Nations, a Georgian who fought with one of the Louisiana regiments. (WTF-9)

FLOYD COUNTY
The Confederate soldier on the right, Thomas Asbury, served in the 8th Regiment, Georgia Volunteer Infantry, and the 1st Regiment, Georgia Volunteer Cavalry. The soldier who posed with him has not been identified. (FLO-151)

Signor Filippo Governale's violin class at Brenau College in Gainesville, ca. 1900. (HAL-135)

C. W. Motes of Atlanta, formerly of Athens, photographed this handsome quartet from Atlanta University in 1894. The original print has been preserved in the university's archives. The musicians are, from the left, Robert W. Gadsden, Joseph T. Porter, George A. Towns, and James Weldon Johnson, later to become famous as a poet. (FUL-214)

RABUN COUNTY

Photographers frequently offered us a chance at our dreams. Howell Lamar Thompson, home on leave from the war in 1918, posed for this studio portrait that shows a soldier trying to be a cowboy. (RAB-229)

SUMTER COUNTY

Facing page: The patriotism generated by war is inevitably seen in portraits of the period. In this photograph taken at the time of World War I or just after, Mary Charlotte Tyson poses with her two brothers, George and E. J., one dressed as a sailor, the other as a soldier, authentic from doughboy cap to canvas leggings. (SUM-148)

MUSCOGEE COUNTY
This lovely bride was photographed in Columbus, probably in the early years of the century. (MUS-147)

BURKE COUNTY
Facing page: Appropriate props and scenery created an "at home" atmosphere in the studio where three generations of women posed for this intimate portrait, ca. 1913. Grandmother Marion Pickens Cole holds granddaughter Marion Neely while the mother, Louise Phinizy Neely, looks on. (BUR-32)

On the following pages:

PUTNAM COUNTY
Left: Tom Thumb wedding, early 1900s. The idea for such "weddings," in which children dressed up as bride, groom, bridesmaids, and so forth, goes back to the wedding of Charles Stratton, better known as "General Tom Thumb," P. T. Barnum's famous midget. (PUT-184)

GWINNETT COUNTY
Right: Gwinnett County chain gang, 1920. (GWN-159)

Two children dressed alike and seated in identical rockers hold onto their dolls while they wait to hear that the photographer has finished taking their picture, ca. 1900. (ROC-136)

R. G. Hollingsworth and his brother Jesse posed in their goat cart for this 1912 picture taken in the yard of the Hollingsworth home in the Spring Hill district of Grady County. The boys held the pose long enough to keep from blurring the picture, but the goats were less cooperative. (GRA-8)

EMANUEL COUNTY
Augustus and Nancy Cowart look straight into the lens of the camera in this ca. 1897 portrait reminiscent of Grant Wood's *American Gothic.* (EMN-28)

COWETA COUNTY
Facing page: In the early years of photography the photographer was sometimes called into the home to capture the likeness of the sick or the invalid. This woman photographed by S. F. Jackson of Newnan in the 1890s lies under a patchwork "crazy quilt," pictures of family members placed beside her. (COW-114)

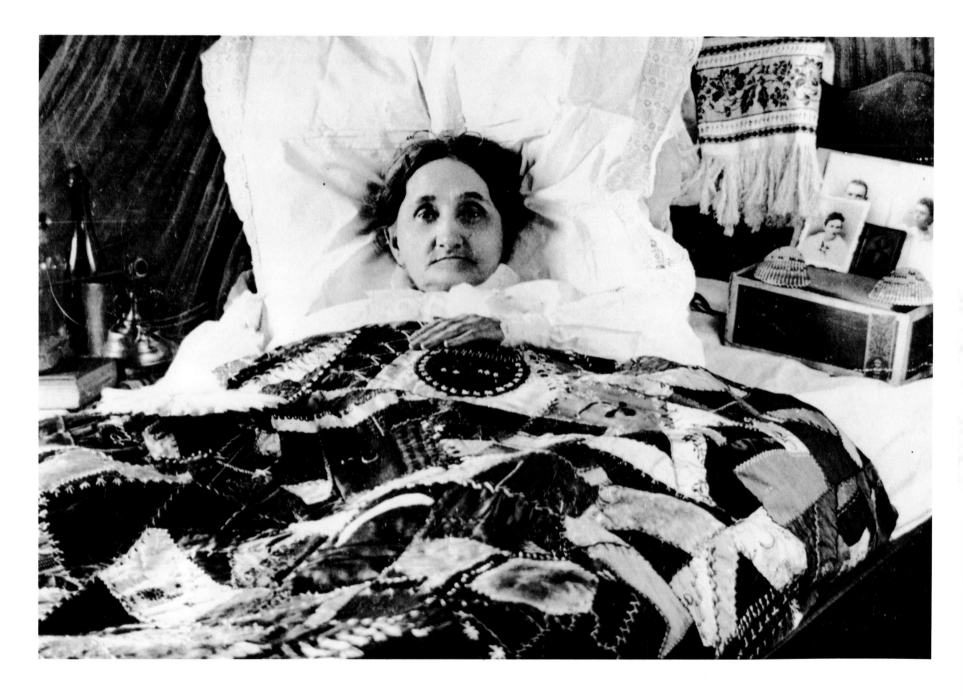

IRWIN COUNTY
Photographers could usually count on a good business from Georgians who visited Civil War battlefields and other points of interest. These three had their picture taken at a spot in present-day Jefferson Davis Memorial Park where Davis, who served as president of the Confederate States of America, was captured by Union troops in 1865 while fleeing south from Richmond. (BEN-179)

GLYNN COUNTY
Old Sibby, a former slave and one of the last
midwives in the area, was photographed in the
Petersville community, 1934. These hands
"caught" many a baby. (GLY-174)

ROCKDALE COUNTY
One of the brotherhood, Monastery of the Holy
Ghost, Conyers. This photograph was taken in
1944, the year the monastery was founded. The
brotherhood resided in a large barn until better
quarters were built. (ROC-21)

FRANKLIN COUNTY
Facing page: Seven of the twelve children of
Benjamin and Mary Vandiver lived into old age
and gathered for this portrait, ca. 1923.
(FRA-170)

FLOYD COUNTY

Steve Eberhart, who had been a slave in the years before the Civil War, in old age became a "regular" at annual gatherings of Confederate veterans. In a 1921 article the Rome newspaper referred to him as "the ancient Senegambian who dresses up in flags and feathers, mostly just before Confederate reunion time." (FLO-38)

FLOYD COUNTY

Facing page: Lee Ella Smith Sparks, Rome, 1895. Leg-of-mutton sleeves were very much in fashion when this picture was taken. (FLO-59)

DECATUR COUNTY

In the late 1880s George Eastman revolutionized photography by putting a camera in everyone's hands. This photograph of three young men, ca. 1890, was taken with the first Kodak, a camera with roll film that had to be sent back to the company for the pictures to be developed and printed. Images taken by early Kodak cameras were circular. (DEC-163)

EMANUEL COUNTY

Mrs. Elizabeth Durden and her grandson, Verdie Ricks, photographed on the front porch of
their home, Norristown, ca. 1900. (EMN-5)

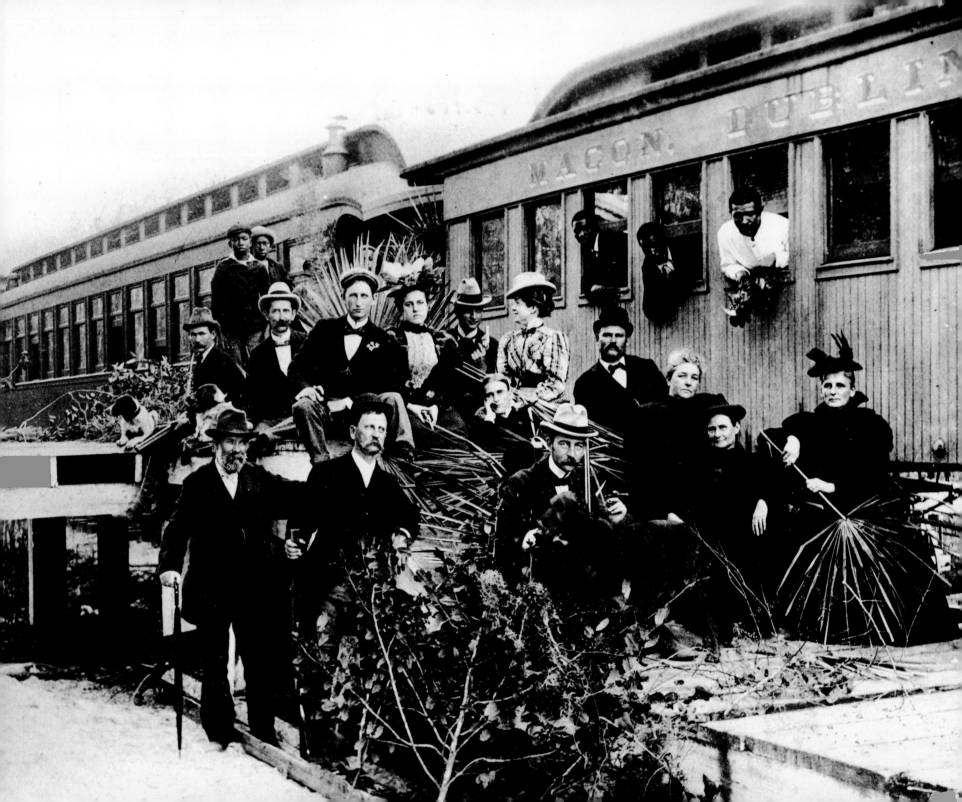

Enjoying Ourselves

There were so many ways to enjoy ourselves. We could hunt, fish, saddle the horse and ride down to the river, go swimming, go on hayrides and picnics. We could dance until the cows came home, and sing ourselves hoarse at camp meetings.

Much of our work around the farm and home provided opportunities for socializing. We got together for barn-raisings, corn-shuckings, quilting bees, and canning parties. As automobiles arrived on the scene, we collected our friends for a leisurely outing.

For many of us social activity centered around the church. After Sunday school and the preacher's sermon we frequently stayed on for all-day church meetings, song fests, and bountiful dinners on the grounds. The women of the family prepared their favorite dishes, be it fried chicken, baked ham, potato salad, apple pie, or peach cobbler. The children played games while the men discussed politics, the weather, and the price of cotton.

Those of us who were able to travel to other parts of the state or to nearby states enjoyed a pleasant summer vacation. Groups rode the train to spend a week or two in the popular resort areas of north Georgia. We took snapshots of Tallulah Falls and Lookout Mountain. Others boarded the Central of Georgia to bask in the sun at Tybee Island.

Political rallies and reunions of one kind or another were always occa-

TWIGGS COUNTY
In the late 1890s and early 1900s the Macon, Dublin and Savannah Railroad, which never got as far as Savannah, ran excursions from Macon to Gallemore's Mill for picnics and outings. This photograph taken in 1899 shows a party about to board the train after just such an outing. The gentleman in the center on the front row is James T. Wright, general manager of the railroad; standing to his right is Colonel Dudley M. Hughes, the M.D.&S.'s first president. (BIB-50)

sions for celebration. We dressed in our best clothes and made our way to the public square where we unveiled monuments to Revolutionary and Civil War heroes and city founders. Politicians, especially those on the state level, launched their campaigns with all-day barbecues that were always well attended. Eugene Talmadge opened his 1932 gubernatorial campaign with a barbecue in Telfair County that took literally weeks to prepare. The barbecue committee enlisted a hundred women and over fifty men to work on barbecue day. Farmers from around the county donated pigs, goats, and cows to make the 10,000 pounds of barbecue and 1,000 pounds of stew that were served.

Young and old alike looked forward to the circuses and carnivals that came to town. We watched the circus parade and followed the colorful wagons to the pasture or vacant lot where the big canvas tent had sprouted. When the carnivals came we rode merry-go-rounds and ferris wheels and paid ten cents to gawk at such wonders as the Wild Aztec Girls and the world's fattest fat lady.

At the annual county fair we could see the latest advances in technology for the home and farm. We entered our finest hogs, our prize cattle and calves in the contests. We vied for blue ribbons with our cakes, pies, canning techniques, and quilts. Children bobbed for apples, competed in pie-eating contests, and tried their skill at spitting watermelon seeds.

We played games of every kind—croquet, golf, basketball, tennis. Everyone loved the Great American Pastime—baseball—and every town had at least one team of its own. School football teams competed with teams from neighboring communities.

As hard as we worked, we found time to have fun. Whether it was a Fourth of July picnic, a day at the fair, or an afternoon on the front porch, we enjoyed ourselves to the fullest.

WHITFIELD COUNTY

The Kirkpatrick family and friends enjoy a leisurely game of croquet in the yard of their home near Varnell, ca. 1890. The scene was carefully staged by the photographer at a time when any motion could spoil the picture. (WTF-239)

Facing page: Lookout Mountain near Chattanooga was conveniently close and therefore a favorite vacation spot for many Georgians. In this photograph taken about 1915 the Lovvorn and Barrow families of Carroll County, like hundreds before them, pose on Umbrella Rock. (CAR-32)

124

GLYNN COUNTY

The King Edwards Trained Wild Animal Arena visits Sea Island, ca. 1900. The two men manage to look both dignified and absurd, one mounted on a donkey, the other astride a camel. (GLY-250)

WILKES COUNTY

Facing page: Photographer J. W. Stephenson captured this moment at a carnival on the square in Washington, ca. 1901. (WLK-119)

GRADY COUNTY

Pelham and Havana Railroad transporting a Cairo Sunday school class to a picnic site, 1913. It is not clear whether these flatcars were being pushed or pulled and therefore whether the handsomely outfitted ladies are facing frontwards or backwards, but the smoke that can be seen to the far right is probably coming from the engine. (GRA-69)

PUTNAM COUNTY

Facing page: Harness racing at the county fair in Eatonton, 1910. The winner of this race was the local favorite, Amourette. Special trains brought crowds from Athens, Macon, and other towns around the state, and between races they were entertained by "Joe Joker," the trotting ostrich, and "Uncle Dan" Boyington's fourteen trained mules. (PUT-151)

WILKES COUNTY

Carefully arranged on the roof, the hood, the fender, and the back bumper of their Peach Belt Lines bus, a touring group from Macon stops to pose for a picture in Washington, ca. 1930. (WLK-16)

FULTON COUNTY

Facing page: "Shooting the Chute." One of the most popular rides at the Cotton States and International Exposition held in Atlanta in 1895 carried fair-goers down a slide and into the lake. The site of the exposition was Piedmont Park. From a stereoscopic view by B. W. Kilburn. (FUL-666)

DECATUR COUNTY

If there was anything funnier than a 149¾-pound watermelon (at least, to the photographer) it was a 304-pound black man about to cut into a 149¾-pound watermelon. Actually what we see in this ca. 1905 picture is two stereotypes coming together: the jolly fat man with an eye for big helpings and the black who couldn't resist watermelon. (DEC-64)

Facing page: In the early years of the century few occasions seemed more filled with fun—at least, in the photographs—than a watermelon cutting. "Face in the rind, now . . . everybody smile . . . hold it . . ." (GEO-114)

Vice, 1918 style. Charlie Miller, Jay Gordon, and Billy Owen amuse themselves by posing for a picture that shows them engaged in two of the vices of the day—smoking and playing cards. But the cigarettes are unlit, the table is too small to accommodate a game of poker, and the photographer's painted backdrop gives the joke away. (GOR-221)

Facing page: If mothers wanted to see what their sons and daughters were doing up in Athens in 1910, they could study this picture. Dancing is one of the vices parodied by these University of Georgia students, as is cheating. (CLR-75)

FULTON COUNTY
In the early years of the century every town had at least one baseball team. Fire departments
had their own teams, and so did high schools and colleges. Pictured here is the Fulton Bag and
Cotton Mill team, Atlanta, 1910. (FUL-678)

How 'bout them Dawgs! Forerunners of modern-day Georgia Bulldogs, ca. 1898. (CLR-146)

A Big 7 Passenger Halladay in the Albany, Ga. Chautauqua Floral Parade

DOUGHERTY COUNTY

Parades were a popular event long before the coming of the automobile, but early automobiles gave them a special flavor. This seven-passenger Halladay was decorated from bow to stern for a Chautauqua floral parade held in Albany, ca. 1910. (DGH-64)

MUSCOGEE COUNTY

Dining room of the steamboat *Pactolus*, 1887. In the days of river travel the *Pactolus* made
regular trips on the Chattahoochee between Columbus and Apalachicola, Florida. (MUS-4)

COBB COUNTY

Circus parade, Marietta, ca. 1910. The parade through the town was designed to generate excitement in those who were wavering, and it usually did. Here, a band is playing atop the circus wagon drawn by white horses. (COB-240)

LUMPKIN COUNTY
The day two Frenchmen brought their dancing bears to town, Dahlonega, 1892. (LUM-58)

The Cow Horn Club, 1901. Members were Civil War veterans who lived near each other and who blew a cow horn to gather and drink mint juleps. (RIC-156)

HALL COUNTY
Facing page: The Sea Shore Girls, ca. 1911. In the early 1900s girls from towns and cities along the coast formed a club at Brenau College. Here they are about to enjoy a swim in a lake on the Gainesville campus. (HAL-178)

On the following pages:

CHATHAM COUNTY
Left: International Road Races sanctioned by the Automobile Club of America drew thousands to Savannah in 1908, 1910, and 1911. This photograph taken at the Grand Prize race course November 27, 1911, shows the judges' grandstand, the start-finish line, and the EMF-30 driven by Tiedeman Trophy-winner Frank Witt. The main event of the day was the Vanderbilt Cup Race, which was won by Ralph Mulford, driving a Lozier. Three days later David Bruce-Brown, driving a big red Fiat, won the Grand Prize Race. Distance: 411.36 miles. Time: 5 hours and 31 minutes. (CTM-65)

MUSCOGEE COUNTY
Right: Members of the Columbus Motorcycle Club line up in front of the Columbus Motor Car Company, ca. 1909. The only woman in the picture is Mrs. John Will Johnson, seated in the sidecar of her husband's motorcycle, fifth from right. (MUS-151)

LUMPKIN COUNTY
Moonshine still near Porter Springs, 1899. This still may have been the source of what the editors of the *Dahlonega Signal* referred to in their columns as "mountain razzle dazzle." (LUM-14)

TATTNALL COUNTY
Facing page: Thompson family reunion, ca. 1900. People looked forward to occasions
such as this to visit with friends and cousins and to sample an abundance of country cooking.
(TAT-73)

WARE COUNTY
Motorcyclists photographed before a race in Waycross, ca. 1914. (WAR-136)

RABUN COUNTY

The mountains of North Georgia beckoned for those who enjoyed hiking, picnicking, and communing with nature. This rather serious group photographed at the turn of the century includes one gentleman who brought along his camera. (RAB-21)

CLARKE COUNTY

Carnivals usually drew large crowds as they moved from town to town, and none of the carnival attractions was more popular than the freak show. There one could gaze upon such living wonders as fire breathers, sword swallowers, two-headed calves, human pincushions. This revolting wonder with a live snake in his mouth was photographed at a carnival in Athens in 1900. (CLR-96)

DEKALB COUNTY

Sightseeing buses at Stone Mountain, 1929. The carving of General Robert E. Lee had been unveiled April 9, 1928, the anniversary of Lee's surrender at Appomattox. The figure of Jefferson Davis had begun to take shape, but that of Stonewall Jackson had not yet been started. (COB-162b)

TERRELL COUNTY

The minstrel show, a form of entertainment that featured white performers in blackface, was immensely popular in the nineteenth century and still enjoyed some popularity as late as the 1920s, when this picture was taken. The young minstrel man is George Thornton Lee, Jr. (TER-6)

LUMPKIN COUNTY

Facing page: Crowd of onlookers at a fiddlers' convention in Dahlonega, 1905. The man doing the fiddling is W. H. Satterfield. (LUM-186)

On the following pages:

COBB COUNTY

Left: Hunting party and their kill from a two-day outing: 192 birds. Left to right, Hiram B. Wade, Guy Roberts, and Judge Newt Morris pose with their dogs in front of the courthouse at Marietta, 1910. (COB-689)

DOUGHERTY COUNTY

Right: C. D. "Catfish" Smith, right, and his brother bring proof of a nice day's catch into the studio of photographer Holland in Albany, ca. 1895. Hunters came too—ready to pose with every kind of game from deer to ducks and wild turkeys. (DGH-83)

H.B. WADE   GUY ROBERTS   JUDGE NEWT MORRIS

Into the Twentieth Century

Automobiling on a country road somewhere in Georgia in the early 1900s. The arrival of the automobile was not universally greeted with enthusiasm. In Gwinnett County, for example, a 1906 law required that any driver approaching a horse or mule "shall bring his machine to a full stop at least one hundred yards from said horse or mule, and shall shut off all his machinery and stop all noise being made by same until said horse or mule has passed his machine and is at least fifty yards beyond." (GEO-112)

The twentieth century did not exactly burst forth on the Georgia scene. Rather, it arrived quietly, so much so that a decade had passed before many Georgians even acknowledged the new era.

Nevertheless, the signs of modernization were there. There had of course been railroads in the state as early as the 1830s. Railroad construction on a large scale had begun in the 1880s, and the railroads continued to grow during the early 1900s, though automobiles and airplanes would eventually reduce them to freight carriers. More and more Georgians were becoming familiar with Henry Ford's Model T, and no longer was the automobile a passing fancy as some thought—a machine designed to frighten the horses. Not long after the turn of the century the Wright brothers, Orville and Wilbur, took to the air at Kitty Hawk and launched the age of aviation. More and more people were beginning to use the telephone and to have their homes wired for electricity.

But it was the automobile that caught and held the public imagination well into the century, and the automobile brought with it many changes: better roads (gravel at first—blacktop and concrete were still in the future), a demand for oil and the products made from it, new habits, and of course an end to old ones. The blacksmith shop gave way to the service station, and the hayride to the drive-in movie.

Farms and farmers felt the effects of industrialization. Improved methods and machinery meant, in some cases, more efficient use of the land. Tractors and combines were slowly replacing horse-drawn implements and equipment. Hundreds of textile mills moved from the Northeast to Georgia and other southern states. Like the rest of the region, Georgia had much to offer, especially an available supply of cheap labor.

The new industry brought badly needed money into the state, but it was the factory worker who paid the price. Working long hard hours for very little pay, the worker felt the frustration of progress in "the New South." Children stood beside their parents in production lines. Labor unions were anathema to these southern folk; nevertheless, one did not have to look too closely to see the bitterness and hostility in their eyes.

Cities and towns grew as they were successful in attracting the new industry. As more and more people came to work, more and more businesses developed to accommodate them. Chain grocery stores appeared. People required medical assistance and legal aid, and doctors, dentists, and attorneys established practices in the communities where they were needed.

One industry above all others symbolized the growth and expansion of the twentieth century—Coca-Cola, the drink that was originally developed as a cure for headaches. Atlanta druggist Asa Griggs Candler bought the rights to the "medicine" in 1887 but soon realized how popular it was among Atlantans as a soft drink. In 1892 he formed the Coca-Cola Company and began setting up bottling companies in every town and city around the state. It was not long before Coca-Cola became the most popular soda in the world.

Modernization proceeded very gradually in the state with one exception: Atlanta grew in every direction. Railroads had made the town, and it was the rail system that enabled Atlanta to serve as the distribution center for the entire Southeast. Industries and factories grew up around the railroads. People came from the rural areas and from other towns and cities to work the new jobs. By the 1940s, Atlanta had far outdistanced any other city in the South.

The twentieth century was a time of transition. It brought new technology, new ideas, new styles and patterns. Many foresaw and took advantage of the changing conditions, while others clung to the past. As Georgia moved into the second half of the century, this dichotomy of new versus old became more and more apparent.

WHITFIELD COUNTY

The first automobile in Dalton, a 1903 Oldsmobile owned by Henry L. Smith. Neither the driver nor the passengers appear to be suffering from "automobile frown," an affliction of the time said to result from "fear of accident, which includes injuries to the machine by explosion." One Georgia newspaper warned that "excessive automobiling means a loss of vitality." (WTF-231)

CLARKE COUNTY

Facing page: Not long after the turn of the century Athens busied itself with plans for the Athens Wheat and Oat Fair, which opened July 9, 1901, with ceremonies on College Avenue. When night came, the crowd was dazzled by the city's street lighting. (CLR-68)

MUSCOGEE COUNTY

At the Columbus Fairgrounds stunts were sometimes staged to entertain the crowd while advertising one of the automobile maker's products. Here, ca. 1921, Charles H. Jenkins demonstrates
the durability of Triplex Springs by taking to the air in his Overland. (MUS-137)

FULTON COUNTY

Employees gather in front of the White Star Automobile Company in Atlanta, ca. 1909. According to the identification written on the negative, these are the first two models of the car from the South's first automobile factory. The White Star carried a driver and one passenger and was powered by a two-cylinder engine. (FUL-427)

COWETA COUNTY
Early fender bender. By 1920 the toll from automobile accidents had risen to the point that a Florida senator took the floor to vow that he would vote to "acquit a man who drew his pistol and shot down a reckless driver." (COW-118)

PULASKI COUNTY
Facing page: Mobley's Garage and Machine Works, the first service station and automobile repair shop in Hawkinsville, 1917. The owner, A. M. Mobley, stands near the gasoline pump holding his daughter. (PUL-10)

163

BURKE COUNTY

An Augusta doctor ditched his automobile after
running down a pedestrian on the road just outside Waynesboro, May 2, 1912. Mrs. Aurelia T.
Jones, the elderly widow of a local judge, became panic-stricken as the machine approached
and ran in front of it. Mrs. Jones later died from
her injuries. (BUR-157)

MORGAN COUNTY

Facing page: This gaily decorated automobile
paraded through the streets of Madison for the
unveiling of a Revolutionary War statue, June
1913. The gentleman standing to the rear of
the car is H. H. Fitzpatrick, Sr.
(MOR-009-005)

On the following pages:

GWINNETT COUNTY

Left: Lawrenceville, 1915. These well-dressed
and wonderfully serious ladies are in fact par-
ticipating in an advertising gimmick. In a
moment they will get off of the boards on
which they are standing and the layer cake
which has been flattened by their weight will
promptly rise—a testimonial to the Majestic
Range in which it was baked and to the salesman who came up with the idea. (GWN-259)

RABUN COUNTY

Right: Home economics class at the Rabun Gap
Industrial School, 1905. (RAB-136)

COLQUITT COUNTY
Pay day at the telephone office in Moultrie, ca. 1900. The operators at the switchboard are too busy to pose for the camera. (CLQ-198)

Turn-of-the-century stenography class. The students are taking notes from a dictating machine. (GEO-31)

WHITFIELD COUNTY

Dalton boosters, 1914. The advent of modern highways offered commercial opportunities to towns along the route. Dalton and Rome competed for the reward of having U.S. Highway 41 come through their towns, and Dalton won the cup for sending the larger motorcade to Chattanooga. It also won the highway. (WTF-273)

TROUP COUNTY

Facing page: With the coming of the automobile came the need for better roads—and eventually for modern highways. Convict labor was often used in state and county road construction. This photograph dates from the mid-1920s. (TRP-193)

On the following pages:

HARRIS COUNTY

Left: Construction of Goat Rock Dam on the Chattahoochee River north of Columbus, 1912. (HRR-1)

BIBB COUNTY

Right: This mammoth arch of cotton bales— over three hundred in all—was erected on Second Street in Macon to welcome President William Howard Taft. On November 4, 1909, Taft rode through the city in an open carriage and passed under the arch on his way to deliver an address at the Macon State Fair. (BIB-167)

GOAT ROCK DEVELOPMENT

GENERAL VIEW FROM EAST SIDE

APRIL 25TH, 1912.

COBB COUNTY
Hupp Special driven by Gus Coleman, the unofficial champion of black race-car drivers in the South, ca. 1922. (COB-276)

CLARKE COUNTY
Facing page: Ben T. Epps built this flying machine in the back of his garage in Athens four years after the historic flight of the Wright brothers. The plane was powered by a two-cylinder motorcycle engine. On its maiden flight in 1907 it soared thirty feet into the air but then slipped sideways and crashed. Epps was killed in the crash of a plane he was piloting thirty years later. (CLR-143)

Local-option elections on Prohibition were serious business but they gave citizens a chance to get together at county courthouses to sing and to socialize as well as to argue the pros and cons. This 1907 photograph was taken at the courthouse in Valdosta, where the ladies, determined to close the saloons, formed a double line four feet apart through which the voters had to pass. When the votes were counted the "Prohis," as they were called, had won by nearly three to one. (LOW-104)

BIBB COUNTY

This display at the Georgia State Exposition in Macon, 1928, featured a "modern" rural kitchen complete with sink, gas range, and hot water heater. (BIB-2)

Starrett Brothers, Inc., Builders
Schultze & Weaver, Architects
Atlanta Biltmore Hotel
Reeves Photo, Atlanta, Ga.

FULTON COUNTY
Atlanta Biltmore Hotel under construction on West Peachtree Street, October 1923.
(FUL-188)

COBB COUNTY
Facing page: Interior of the Coca-Cola Bottling Company in Marietta, ca. 1910. (COB-443)

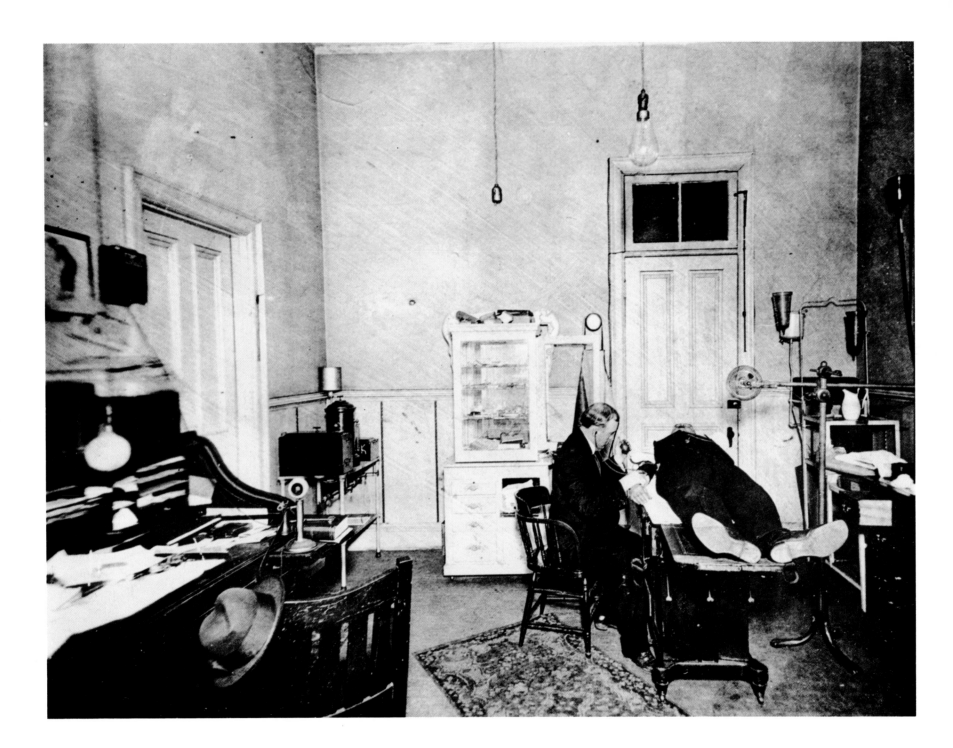

Young dentist, 1909. This photograph shows
Dr. R. R. Douglas working on a patient not
long after he began to practice in Wrightsville.
(JHN-113)

Facing page: Dr. William C. Thompson check-
ing a patient's blood pressure in his Dublin office,
ca. 1911. The doctor's office was well equipped
for its time. (LAU-191)

RICHMOND COUNTY

Busy Broad Street in Augusta, ca. 1929. The marquee of the Imperial Theater, in the block to the right beyond the *Herald* Building, advertises "Singing and Talking Pictures." (RIC-33)

DOUGHERTY COUNTY

In 1929 *Pardners*, a movie promoting forest-fire prevention, was filmed in Georgia. This photograph shows the cast and crew on the set in Dougherty County at the wrap-up of the picture.
The film was shown in other southern states as well as Georgia. (DGH-121)

First telephone in Lawrenceville, ca. 1902. The first call in any town was an event to be recorded. (GWN-239)

COFFEE COUNTY

Small towns vied for the honor of being selected stopping points on a Round-the-State Tour by automobile enthusiasts in October 1910. This photograph shows several of the machines stopped in Douglas for a dinner break before cranking up and heading for the next town on the eight-day tour. When Atlanta's contingency of thirty-five cars pulled into Douglas, local Chamber of Commerce secretary Charles O. DuVall was at the head of the pack, driving his new 60-horsepower Thomas Flyer, Coffee County's "Booster Car." (COF-84)

On the following pages:

DOUGHERTY COUNTY

Left: Agricultural science class at Albany State College, 1923. The school began as the dream of Joseph Winthrop Holley, a young black minister and educator who founded the Albany Manual Training and Agricultural Institute in 1903 in the rear of a dilapidated church building. At the beginning of the century educational opportunities for blacks were sadly limited. (DGH-135)

GLYNN COUNTY

Right: Airship Squadron ZP2 in hangar no. 1 at the Glynco Naval Air Station near Brunswick, ca. 1943. The blimps were used to spot German submarines off the Georgia, Florida, and South Carolina coasts during World War II. (GLY-106)

Days Remembered

Unlike any other medium, photography can capture those special occasions and events that live on in our minds long after they occur.
One glance at a photograph can rekindle our memories and reawaken our
past. It can bring back the thoughts, feelings, even the sounds and smells
of those particular moments from years gone by.

The occasions that were recorded ranged from those with purely per-
sonal significance to those of national importance—from the day we took
our first communion or celebrated our golden wedding anniversary to the
day we watched FDR's body being taken from the Little White House to
the Warm Springs depot where the funeral train waited. The days had
something in common: they were days we would never forget.

So many of the photographs recorded our rites of passage. The camera
caught our mischievous grins as we posed with our classmates in front of
the school. It documented our most solemn expressions as we were baptized in the cool waters of the nearest creek or river. It preserved our
proud and contented faces on our graduation day, and the smiles that hid
the butterflies in our stomachs the day of our wedding.

The camera also captured those tragic events caused by nature. It re-
vealed the massive destruction caused by a tornado or hurricane and con-
veyed the pain and loss felt by those who survived to rebuild. It showed
the town under three feet of water after the river overflowed. It caught

the sense of helplessness we felt as the courthouse went up in flames and we lost forever deeds to the land our families had lived on for generations.

The camera also recorded our hates, our fears, and our prejudices. It showed how some of us posed, even proudly, beside the body of a man whom a mob had just lynched. Some of us cried out. Others could not for fear of being next.

In our family albums we collected pictures of important days in the life of our community. We used our cameras to record the "firsts" in our town —the first automobile, the first streetcar, the first firetruck, the first street paving. We gathered around to witness the very first telephone call being made from our county.

We took photos to remember those never-to-be repeated events that generated so much excitement in our lives. With the camera we captured forever the day the elephant trampled its keeper to death and went stampeding through the town. The police chief finally killed the animal and then, rifle in hand, posed atop his prize to preserve this special moment. We ran outside to take pictures the day the plane's engine failed, forcing it to land in our neighbor's field. We made photographs the day the hot-air balloon took off outside of town.

Indeed it was a special occasion when colorful politicians such as Eugene Talmadge visited our community. We brought cameras to document the glimpse we hoped to catch of President Taft when he visited Macon, to record the fire in Tom Watson's eyes as he spoke in Washington, Georgia, or to cheer Hoke Smith on to victory in Fitzgerald.

We took photographs to remember the days we sent fathers, sons, and brothers off to war. And we took even more to remember the day they returned. These photographs reflect not only what we did and how we did it, but moments we deemed worthy of preserving.

FULTON COUNTY
Christmas in Atlanta, ca. 1900. Despite the dolls and the tree decorated with candles and ornaments, this photograph of the Robert Murdoch Walker family records what seems to be a somber occasion. From a glass plate negative. (FUL-695-82)

FULTON COUNTY

Rare stereoscopic view of Atlanta during the Civil War, from a series published by E. and H. T. Anthony. The building to the right is the railroad station, which was destroyed by Sherman's army in 1864 shortly after this picture was taken. (FUL-597)

FULTON COUNTY

Facing page: Ruins of the railroad roundhouse in Atlanta, 1864. This photograph was taken by Union army photographer George N. Barnard and published in his *Photographic Views of Sherman's Campaign.* Although Sherman left Atlanta in ruins before his famous march to the sea, the destruction of the roundhouse was the work of Confederate forces fleeing the city before him. (FUL-156)

Providence Spring on the site of the Anderson-
ville prison, 1896. The spring provided fresh
water for Union soldiers imprisoned at Ander-
sonville during the Civil War, and many con-
sidered the water a gift from heaven—hence
the name. Veterans who visited the Anderson-
ville site in the years after the war returned to
the spring. (SUM-152)

THOMAS COUNTY
Facing page: Snowstorms such as the one that
hit Thomasville in 1895 were events worthy of
being recorded. The three gentlemen in the
horse-drawn sled were photographed in front of
the popular Piney Woods Hotel. (THO-249)

RICHMOND COUNTY
The Albion Hotel fire in downtown Augusta, November 26, 1921. The fire destroyed half a
block on Broad Street. (RIC-22)

GORDON COUNTY
Facing page: Automobiles converge on Calhoun for the parade and festivities connected with
the opening of the "Dixie Highway" between Atlanta and Chattanooga, 1928. (GOR-332)

THOMAS COUNTY
World War I troop train photographed during a stop at Thomasville, ca. 1917. (THO-134)

GRADY COUNTY
Facing page: Citizens of Cairo congregate downtown to celebrate the signing of the Armistice and the end of World War I, 1918. There were similar scenes of rejoicing in other small towns across the state and nation. (GRA-68)

When Gypsy, a circus elephant, trampled her keeper to death on November 22, 1902, and went on a wild rampage through the streets of Valdosta, Chief of Police Calvin Dampier and a posse of citizens spent part of one night tracking the enraged animal. The following day Dampier brought the elephant down with a shot from his rifle. Here he poses atop the dead animal. (LOW-49)

Facing page: Funeral procession for Senator Benjamin H. Hill, Atlanta, August 16, 1882. The funeral cortege has paused for a moment on Whitehall Street. (FUL-10)

GRADY COUNTY

Cairo, 1916. Automobiles decorated with flags parade down Broad Street to celebrate the
Fourth of July. (GRA-416b)

ELBERT COUNTY

Facing page: Stonecutters pose for the photographer in front of the Elberton Granite & Marble
Works, 1903. The man standing just to the left of center of the picture, wearing a derby, is
Peter Bertoni, who started the production of fine monuments in Elberton. The small boy is
Bertoni's son Jim. The source of the photograph was the Elberton Granite Association.
(ELB-21)

BEN HILL COUNTY
Residents of Fitzgerald gather to witness the lift-off of a hot-air balloon, ca. 1900. (BEN-319)

STEPHENS COUNTY
Facing page: Ceremony on the courthouse lawn in Toccoa, November 15, 1922. As the monument erected by the United Daughters of the Confederacy in honor of the Confederate dead was unveiled, a band played "Tenting on the Old Camp Ground" and aged veterans seated on the grandstand rose and gave the Rebel yell. (STP-26)

Lynching of Leo Frank, August 16, 1915. In what became Georgia's most celebrated legal case, Leo Frank, a factory superintendent, was convicted of murdering 14-year-old Mary Phagan, an employee. Governor John Slaton commuted Frank's sentence to life imprisonment, to the dissatisfaction of some Georgians who took their idea of justice into their own hands. They seized Frank from the state prison in Milledgeville, carried him to Marietta, the home of Mary Phagan, and hanged him. (BAL-51)

DECATUR COUNTY

Facing page: Lynching was an ugly form of mob violence that continued into the twentieth century and that was most often directed at blacks. This 1905 photograph shows Gus Goodman, who was taken from the jail in Bainbridge by a mob and hanged after fatally wounding the sheriff. (DEC-87)

Wreck of Canadian Curtis Biplane
Bowden, Feb 21, 1920
C. W. Meyer Pilot
Burt Hood Passenger

TARPLEY
-Photo-

CARROLL COUNTY

In the early days of aviation the appearance of a plane was certain to draw a crowd. This Curtis biplane piloted by C. W. Meyer visited Bowdon on February 21, 1920. The photograph on the facing page shows Meyer and passenger Burt Hood just prior to take-off. On this page they stand beside the wreckage of the plane, which crashed in a thicket of trees a few minutes after they were airborne. (CAR-34, CAR-33)

President Grover Cleveland takes in the sights at the Cotton States and International Exposition in Atlanta, October 1895. The exposition attracted 800,000 visitors. (FUL-674)

BEN HILL COUNTY
Facing page: Politicking was cause for grand celebrations and parades. This band was assembled in front of the Aldine Hotel in Fitzgerald to add excitement to the Hoke Smith campaign, 1906. Smith was elected governor. (BEN-121)

On the following pages:

TROUP COUNTY
Left: Eugene Talmadge on the campaign trail, 1936. Talmadge, who served as Governor of Georgia for four terms, attempted to unseat Senator Richard B. Russell, Jr., but was defeated in the democratic primary. (TRP-321)

MCDUFFIE COUNTY
Right: Tom Watson, one of Georgia's most colorful political figures, speaking to a crowd on the occasion of his departure for Washington, D.C., and the United States Senate, 1921. (MCD-101)

TROUP COUNTY
Smoke engulfs the Troup County courthouse in La Grange during the fire that destroyed it, November 5, 1936. (TRP-202)

HALL COUNTY
Facing page: On the morning of April 6, 1936, two enormous funnels cut through the heart of Gainesville, killing some 150 people, injuring more than 700 others, destroying more than 500 homes, and wreaking havoc in the business district. This photograph was taken in front of the *Gainesville News* building not long after the tornado struck. (HAL-59)

On the following pages:

LUMPKIN COUNTY
Left: Funeral of Captain W. B. Fry, 1912. In the early years of the century the dead were "laid out" in the home, but were frequently taken to the church for a final service. (LUM-203)

LUMPKIN COUNTY
Right: Group being baptized in a lock on the Yahoola Creek, ca. 1925. Early 1900 newspaper accounts of baptismal ceremonies sometimes referred to the number of "submersions." (LUM-98)

HABERSHAM COUNTY

Wreck on the Tallulah Falls Railroad, February 7, 1927. Two people were killed when the 70-foot-high Hazel Creek trestle near Demorest collapsed, sending the engine, the baggage car, and a passenger car plunging into the ravine below. Miraculously, the car in which most of the passengers were riding came to a stop just short of the break in the trestle. (HAB-31)

EMANUEL COUNTY

Facing page: Revenue officers bring in a moonshine still, Swainsboro, ca. 1920. The objects on the fenders of the car are copper coils. (EMN-53)

On the following pages:

GORDON COUNTY

Left: Calhoun, 1942. Fifty-seven men entering military service in World War II pose for a farewell picture before boarding buses. (GOR-389)

BARROW COUNTY

Right: Senator Richard B. Russell, Jr., waves to the crowd that turned out to honor him in his hometown of Winder, 1957. Russell served in the Senate from 1933 until his death in 1971. (BRW-91)

MERIWETHER COUNTY

Hearse carrying the body of Franklin Delano Roosevelt to the funeral train arrives at the Warm Springs depot, April 13, 1945. The president had died the afternoon before at his nearby cottage. The photographer recording this scene also caught his own silhouette reflected in a window of the hearse. (MER-44)

MUSCOGEE COUNTY

Facing page: Fort Benning, 1941. Men prepare for a jump as part of early paratroop training. (MUS-67)